Master Maths at Home

Graphs, Averages and Measuring

Scan the QR code to help your child's learning at home.

DK | MATHS NO PROBLEM!

mastermathsathome.com

How to use this book

Maths — No Problem! created **Master Maths at Home** to help children develop fluency in the subject and a rich understanding of core concepts.

Key features of the Master Maths at Home books include:

- Carefully designed lessons that provide structure, but also allow flexibility in how they're used.

- Speech bubbles containing content designed to spark diverse conversations, with many discussion points that don't have obvious 'right' or 'wrong' answers.

- Rich illustrations that will guide children to a discussion of shapes and units of measurement, allowing them to make connections to the wider world around them.

- Exercises that allow a flexible approach and can be adapted to suit any child's cognitive or functional ability.

- Clearly laid-out pages that encourage children to practise a range of higher-order skills.

- A community of friendly and relatable characters who introduce each lesson and come along as your child progresses through the series.

You can see more guidance on how to use these books at **mastermathsathome.com**.

We're excited to share all the ways you can learn maths!

Copyright © 2022 Maths — No Problem!

Maths — No Problem!
mastermathsathome.com
www.mathsnoproblem.com
hello@mathsnoproblem.com

First published in Great Britain in 2022 by
Dorling Kindersley Limited
One Embassy Gardens, 8 Viaduct Gardens, London SW11 7BW
A Penguin Random House Company

The authorised representative in the EEA is Dorling Kindersley
Verlag GmbH. Arnulfstr. 124, 80636 Munich, Germany

10 9 8 7 6 5 4 3 2 1
001–327106–May/22

A CIP catalogue record for this book is available from the British Library.

ISBN: 978-0-24153-950-7
Printed and bound in the UK

For the curious
www.dk.com

This book was made with Forest Stewardship Council™ certified paper – one small step in DK's commitment to a sustainable future. For more information go to www.dk.com/our-green-pledge

Acknowledgements
The publisher would like to thank the authors and consultants Andy Psarianos, Judy Hornigold, Adam Gifford and Dr Anne Hermanson.

The Castledown typeface has been used with permission from the Colophon Foundry.

Contents

Ruby   Elliott   Amira   Charles   Lulu   Sam   Oak   Holly   Ravi   Emma   Jacob   Hannah

Types of averages

Starter

A baker decorates some cakes using stars. How can we describe the number of stars on the cakes using 1 number?

Example

The **mode**, **median** and **mean** are all averages.

In this set, the mode is 3.

The mode is the number we see most often.

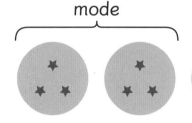

mode

The value 3 appears most often.

In this set, the median is 4.

The median is the middle value once the values are arranged from smallest to greatest or greatest to smallest.

median

In this set, the mean is 5.

3 + 3 + 4 + 7 + 8 = 25
25 ÷ 5 = 5

First, we find the sum of the values.

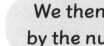

We then divide the sum by the number of values.

When we say 'the average is 5', we often mean that 'the mean is 5.'

Practice

Find the mean number of items in the bowls.

1 ☐ + ☐ + ☐ = ☐

☐ ÷ 3 = ☐

mean = ☐

2 ☐ + ☐ + ☐ + ☐ = ☐

☐ ÷ 4 = ☐

mean = ☐

3 ☐

mean = ☐

Finding the mean (part 1)

Starter

Hannah packed pears into bags so that each bag had a mass of approximately 2 kg. Ravi packed apples into bags so that each bag had a mass of approximately 1 kg.

What is the average number of pieces of fruit that Hannah and Ravi packed into a single bag?

> We are looking for the mean when we say 'average' here.

Example

Find the sum of the set.

9 + 11 + 10 + 12 + 8 = 50

50 ÷ 5 = 10

> Add to find the total number of pears.

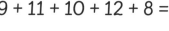

> The average number of pears in a single bag is 10.

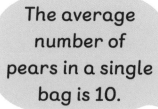

$8 + 11 + 9 + 10 + 11 + 8 = 57$

Find the average number of apples in a single bag.

$57 ÷ 6 = 9.5$

Even though Ravi did not put half an apple in each bag, the average number of apples in a single bag is 9.5.

Practice

Jacob, Charles and Emma bought 5 bouquets of flowers.
Find the average number of flowers in a single bouquet for each child.

1

mean =

2

mean =

3

mean =

Finding the mean (part 2)

Starter

The average number of grapes in the children's lunch boxes is 20. How many grapes are in each child's lunch box?

Example

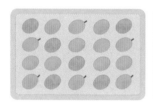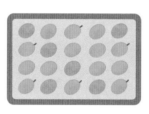

20   20   20

20 + 20 + 20 = 60
60 ÷ 3 = 20
mean = 20

It is possible that each child has the same number of grapes.

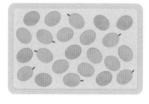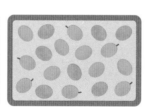

23   18   19

23 + 18 + 19 = 60
60 ÷ 3 = 20
mean = 20

Each lunch box could contain a similar number of grapes.

Is it possible for each lunch box to contain this number of grapes?

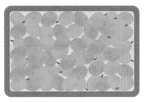

1   1   58

1 + 1 + 58 = 60

60 ÷ 3 = 20

mean = 20

The children are more likely to each have been given a similar number of grapes for their lunch.

Even though the mean of all of the examples are the same, the first two examples are more likely to represent the number of grapes in the lunch boxes.

Practice

1 Three friends each bought a packet of chocolate peanuts.

Complete the table to show 3 different possibilities for the number of pieces in each packet that will give an average of 30 pieces per packet.

	Packet A	Packet B	Packet C
1			
2			
3			

Chocolate Peanuts

Average contents: 30 pieces

2 It is possible that the 3 packets contained the following number of pieces.

Packet A: 1 piece   Packet B: 1 piece   Packet C: 88 pieces

Explain why it is unlikely that this would be the case.

Drawing pie charts

Starter

The table shows the number of goals each football team scored in a tournament. How can this information be shown?

Team	Number of goals
Foxton Flyers (FF)	8
Shorehill Superstars (SS)	12
Greenfield Goalscorers (GG)	8
Townsville Titans (TT)	16
Plymouth Pirates (PP)	4

Example

We can show this information using a bar graph.

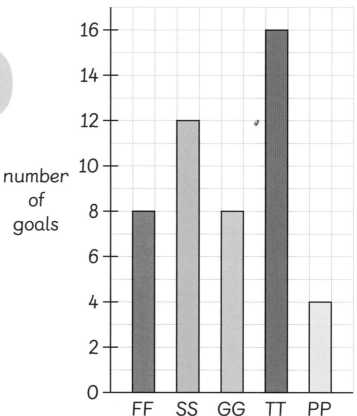

Number of Goals Scored in the Tournament

We can show the same information using a bar model.

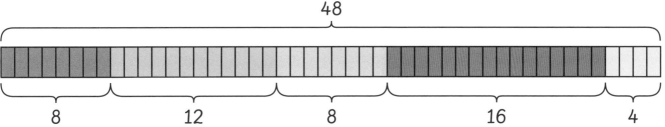

48

8   12   8   16   4

Foxton Flyers: 8 out of 48 goals is equal to $\frac{1}{6}$ of all the goals.

Shorehill Superstars: 12 out of 48 goals is equal to $\frac{1}{4}$ of all the goals.

Greenfield Goalscorers: 8 out of 48 goals is equal to $\frac{1}{6}$ of all the goals.

Townsville Titans: 16 out of 48 goals is equal to $\frac{1}{3}$ of all the goals.

Plymouth Pirates: 4 out of 48 goals is equal to $\frac{1}{12}$ of all of the goals.

This information can also be shown on a pie chart.

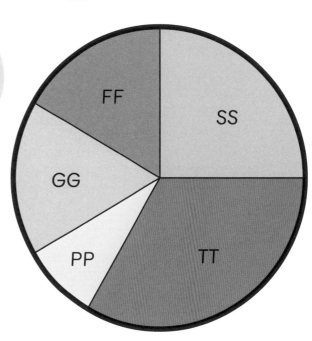

We can write all of the fractions as twelfths so the pie chart is divided into 12 parts.

We can divide the total number of goals by the number of parts on the pie chart to find the value of each part.

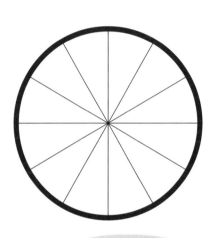

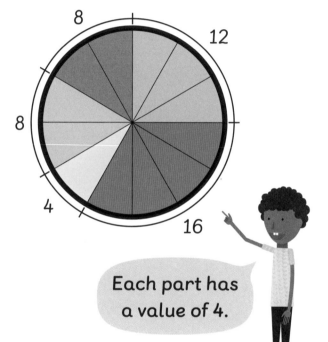

8

12

8

4

16

  $48 \div 12 = 4$

Each part has a value of 4.

Practice

1 The table shows the number of meals sold in a restaurant in one evening. Show the information in the table on the pie chart.

Type of meal	Number of meals sold
lasagne	6
pizza	12
fish and chips	18
macaroni cheese	12

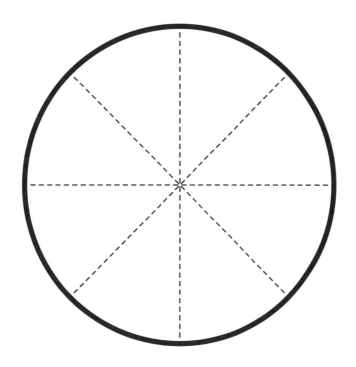

2 The information in the table shows the number of each type of cookie on sale in a bakery. Show the information in the table on the pie chart.

Type of cookie	Number of cookies
milk choc-chip	6
vanilla	3
hazelnut	9
walnut	6
white choc-chip	12

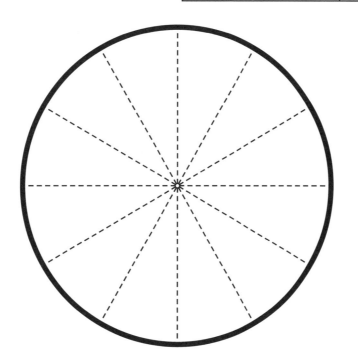

Understanding pie charts (part 1)

Starter

Forty-eight children were asked to choose their favourite sport.
What information can we get from the pie chart?

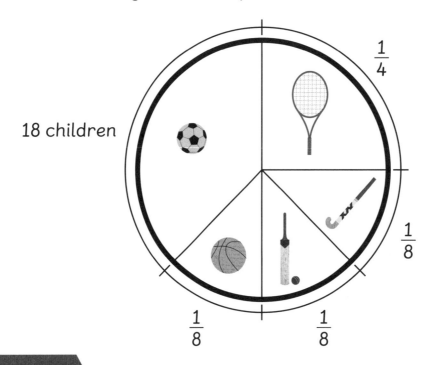

18 children

$\frac{1}{4}$

$\frac{1}{8}$

$\frac{1}{8}$

$\frac{1}{8}$

Example

We know that this represents half or $\frac{4}{8}$ of the children.

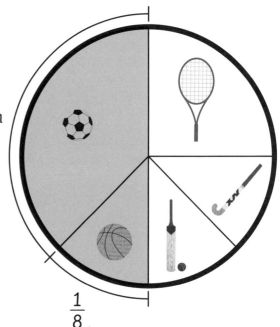

18 children

$\frac{1}{8}$

$$\frac{1}{2} = \frac{4}{8}$$

$$\frac{1}{8} + \frac{3}{8} = \frac{4}{8}$$

18 children chose football as their favourite sport.

We know that 18 children represents $\frac{3}{8}$ of the total number of children.

$$\frac{3}{8} = 18$$

$$\frac{1}{8} = 18 \div 3$$

$$= 6$$

$\frac{1}{8}$ of the children or 6 children chose basketball as their favourite sport.

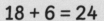

18 + 6 = 24
24 children chose football or basketball as their favourite sport.

If we know that $\frac{1}{2}$ of the pie chart is equal to 24 children, we can find $\frac{1}{4}$ of the total number of children.

$$\frac{1}{2} = 24$$

$$\frac{1}{4} = 24 \div 2$$

$$= 12$$

24 children

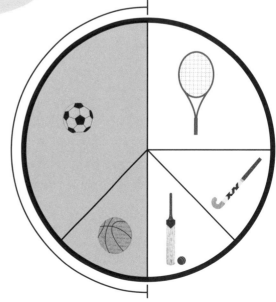

 We can show the children's choices in a table.

Sport	football	basketball	cricket	hockey	tennis
Number of children	18	6	6	6	12

We can show the fraction of the total number of children who chose each sport.

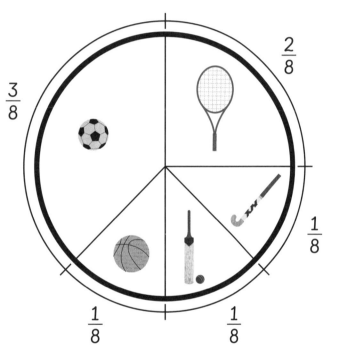

$\frac{3}{8}$

$\frac{2}{8}$

$\frac{1}{8}$

$\frac{1}{8}$

$\frac{1}{8}$

We can show the number of children who chose each sport.

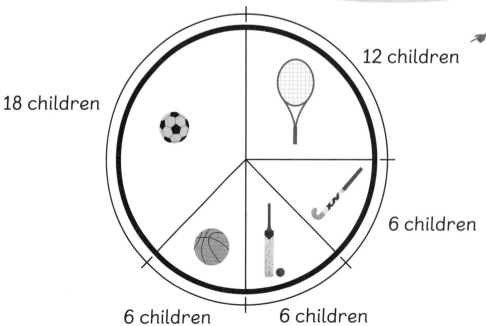

18 children

12 children

6 children

6 children

6 children

The pie chart shows the number of pets that the pupils in Year 6 own.
Use the information given to complete the table.

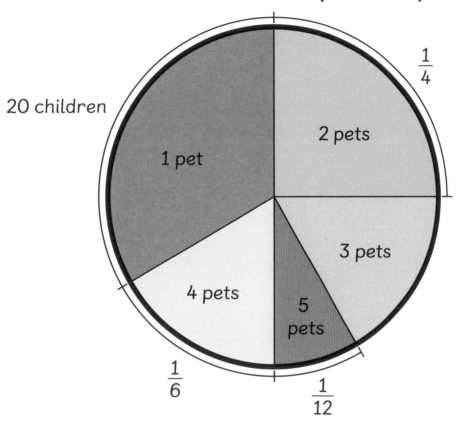

Number of Pets Owned by Year 6 Pupils

Number of pets	1	2	3	4	5
Number of pupils	20				

Understanding pie charts (part 2)

Starter

Sam is making 160 g of herb and spice mix to add to a dish he is cooking.
How many grams of each herb or spice does Sam need?

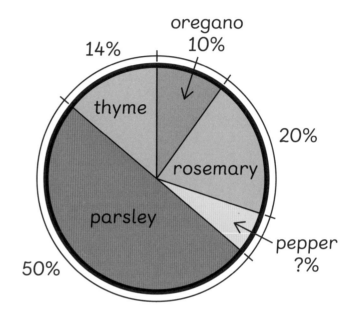

Example

160 g ÷ 2 = 80 g
80 g of the herb and spice mix is parsley.

I know that 50% is equal to $\frac{1}{2}$.

Find the mass of the oregano.

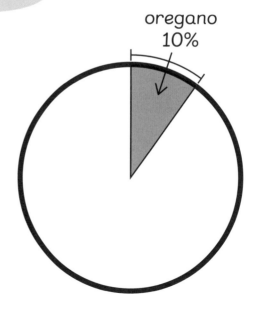

Mass of oregano = 10% of 160 g
160 ÷ 10 = 16
Sam needs 16 g of oregano.

20% is double 10%.

Mass of rosemary = 20% of 160 g
10% of 160 g = 16
20% of 160 g = 16 × 2
             = 32 g
Sam needs 32 g of rosemary.

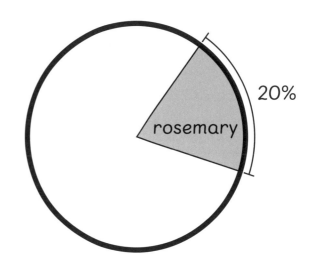

 **We need to find the mass of the pepper.**

10 + 20 + ? + 50 + 14 = 100
10 + 20 + 50 + 14 = 94
100 − 94 = 6
6% of the herb and spice mix is pepper.

 To find 6% we can start by finding 5%.

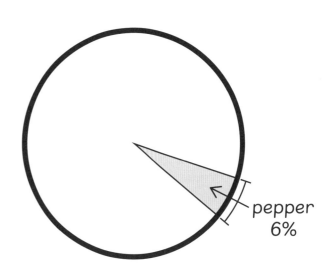

Mass of pepper = 6% of 160 g
10% of 160 g = 16 g
5% of 160 g = 16 ÷ 2
            = 8 g

10% of 160 g = 16 g
1% of 160 g = 16 ÷ 10
            = 1.6 g

Next, we need to find 1%.

8 + 1.6 = 9.6
Sam needs 9.6 g of pepper.

I found 14% of 160 g this way.

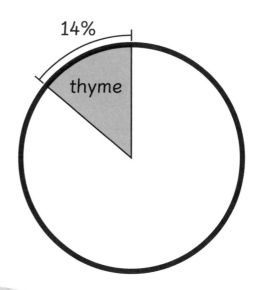

14%

thyme

Mass of thyme = 14% of 160 g
10% of 160 g = 16 g
5% of 160 g = 8 g
1% of 160 g = 1.6 g
4% of 160 g = 8 − 1.6
        = 6.4 g
16 + 6.4 = 22.4

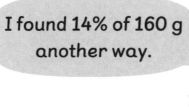

I found 14% of 160 g another way.

10% of 160 g = 16 g
1% of 160 g = 1.6 g
4% of 160 g = 1.6 × 4
        = 6.4 g
16 + 6.4 = 22.4
Sam needs 22.4 g of thyme.

Practice

1 The pie chart shows the types of books in a class library. Complete the table.

Type of book	Percentage of all books
comics	10%
fiction	
reference books	20%
non-fiction	

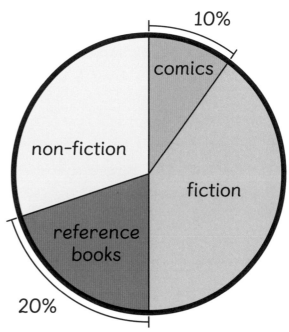

10%

comics

non-fiction

fiction

reference books

20%

2 The pie chart shows the mass of each type of vegetable Ruby used in a salad. Ruby used 140 g of cucumber in the salad. Find the mass of the remaining vegetables.

Mass of Vegetables Used in Ruby's Salad

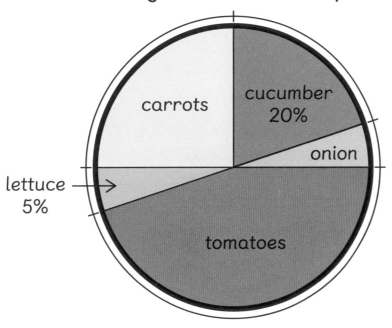

(a) The mass of the lettuce Ruby used was ⬚ g.

(b) The mass of the carrots Ruby used was ⬚ g.

(c) The mass of the onion Ruby used was ⬚ g.

(d) The mass of the tomatoes Ruby used was ⬚ g.

Understanding line graphs (part 1)

Starter

Elliott knows that the water runs from his bath tap at a rate of 10 l every 2 minutes.
He knows it takes 90 l of water to fill the bath. The water has been running for 14 minutes. How much longer does Elliott have to wait until the bath is full?

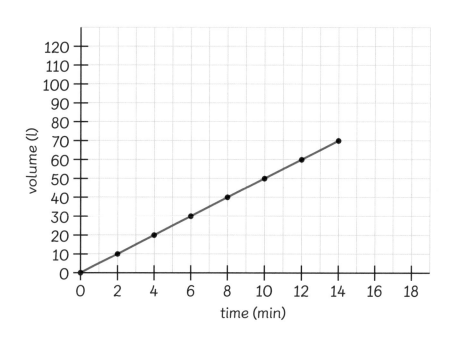

Example

The water is running at a constant rate.

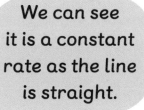

We can see it is a constant rate as the line is straight.

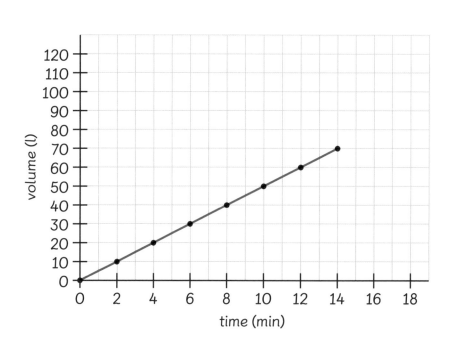

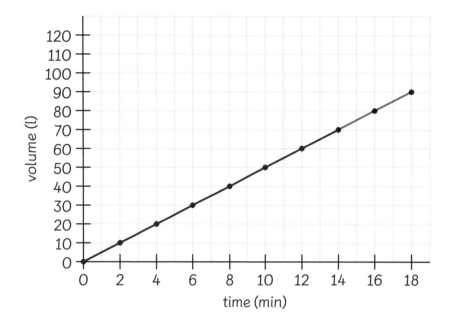

We can predict when the bath will be full by extending the line.

The bath will have 90 l of water in it after 18 minutes.
Elliott will need to wait 4 more minutes until the bath is full.

Practice

The line graph shows the distance travelled by Mr Nightingale when driving his car on a motorway.

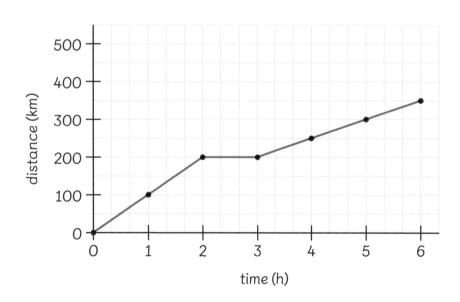

1 The car travelled at ⬚ km per hour during the first 2 hours.

2 For how long was the car not moving due to a traffic jam? ⬚ h

3 The car was driving at 50 km per hour for ⬚ hours.

Understanding line graphs (part 2)

Starter

The line graph shows the number of bread rolls a large bakery produces over a 6-hour shift on a weekday and at the weekend.
What can we say about the rate of production on a weekday and at the weekend?

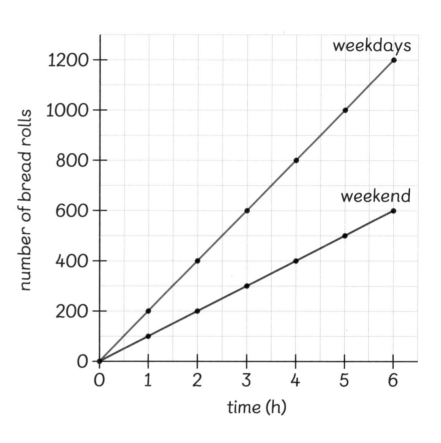

Example

The straight lines show us that the bakery produces bread rolls at a constant rate on a weekday and at the weekend.

The angle of the lines show us that the rate of production on a weekday is greater than the rate of production at the weekend.

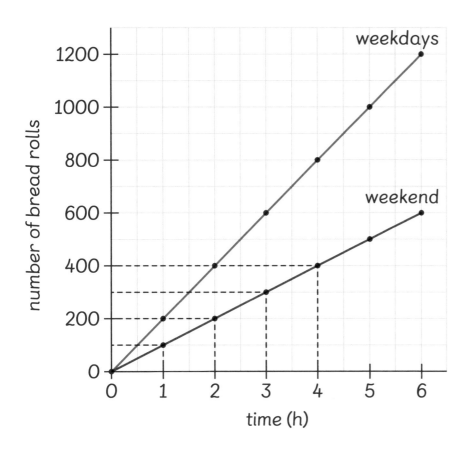

The rate of production during the weekend is 100 bread rolls per hour.
The factory produces twice as many bread rolls per hour on a weekday.

Line graphs can be used to predict an outcome over time.

We can use the line graph to help predict the number of bread rolls that would be made over an 8-hour shift.

Time (h)	0	1	2	3	4	5	6	7	8
Number of bread rolls: weekdays	0	200	400	600	800	1000	1200	1400	1600
Number of bread rolls: weekend	0	100	200	300	400	500	600	700	800

1 The line graph shows the average number of rubbish bins collected in one morning in a small town.

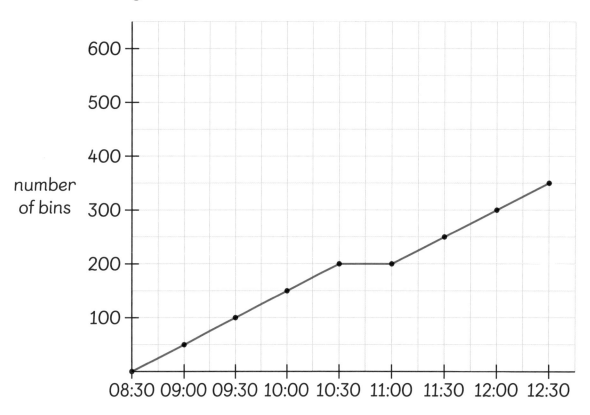

(a) Place the information shown on the line graph in the table below.

Time	08:30	09:00	09:30	10:00	10:30	11:00	11:30	12:00	12:30
Number of bins									

(b) Use the information shown on the graph and in the table to complete the following sentences.

(i) By 10:30, ☐ rubbish bins had been collected.

(ii) By 12:30, ☐ rubbish bins had been collected.

(iii) At ☐ , the workers stopped collecting rubbish bins and had a break.

2 The line graph shows the number of people who rode on two different rollercoasters in one day.

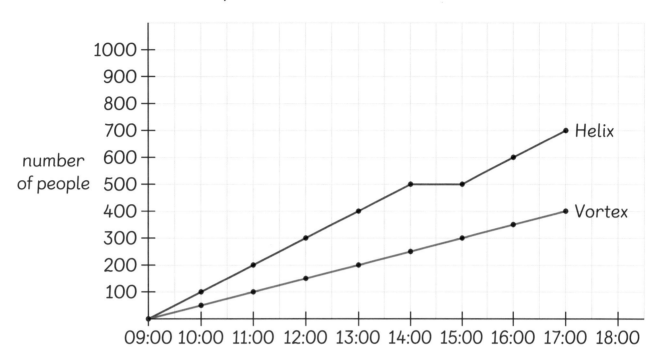

(a) Place the information shown on the line graph in the table below.

Time	09:00	10:00	11:00	12:00	13:00	14:00	15:00	16:00	17:00
Number of people: Helix									
Number of people: Vortex									

(b) Use the information shown on the graph and in the table to answer the following questions.

   (i)   How many more people had ridden the Helix than the Vortex

         by 12:00?

   (ii) How many people per hour rode the Vortex?

   (iii) During the day, the Helix had to close for repairs.

         For how long was the Helix closed?

Converting millimetres and centimetres

Starter

Charles found this image while looking for a new pair of glasses.

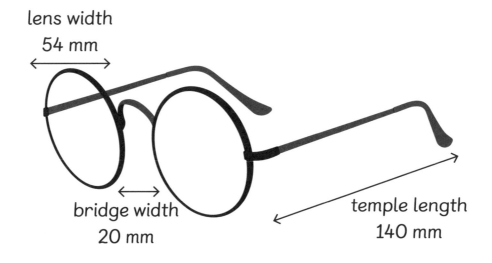

lens width
54 mm

bridge width
20 mm

temple length
140 mm

Can we show the same measurements in centimetres?

Example

Convert 20 mm to cm.

10 mm = 1 cm
1 mm = 0.1 cm

1 mm is 10 times smaller than 1 cm.
1 cm is 10 times greater than 1 mm.

20 mm = 2 cm

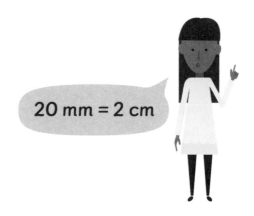

Convert 140 mm to cm.

10 mm = 1 cm
100 mm = 10 cm

140 mm = 14 cm

Convert 54 mm to cm.

10 mm = 1 cm
50 mm = 5 cm
1 mm = 0.1 cm
4 mm = 0.4 cm

54 mm = 5.4 cm

Practice

1 Convert millimetres to centimetres.

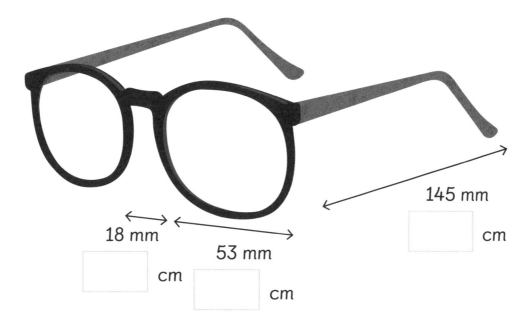

145 mm

☐ cm

18 mm

☐ cm

53 mm

☐ cm

2 Convert the following measurements.

(a) 72 mm = ☐ cm

(b) 4.5 cm = ☐ mm

(c) 10.7 cm = ☐ mm

(d) 209 mm = ☐ cm

Converting centimetres and metres

Starter

Emma knits a hat for one of her toys
using different lengths of coloured wool.
She uses 1.8 m of blue wool.
How many centimetres is this?

Example

1 m = 100 cm
0.1 m = 10 cm
0.8 m = 80 cm

1.8 m = 180 cm

Emma uses 1.8 m or 180 cm of blue wool.

Emma uses 1.35 m
of red wool.

1 m = 100 cm
0.1 m = 10 cm
0.01 m = 1 cm

1 m is 100 times greater than 1 cm.
1 cm is 100 times smaller than 1 m.

1.35 m = 135 cm

Practice

1 Write the lengths of the different coloured wool in centimetres.

(a)

blue wool
4.3 m

☐ cm

(b)

pink wool
4.6 m

☐ cm

(c)

yellow wool
5.2 m

☐ cm

(d)

purple wool
1.62 m

☐ cm

(e)

orange wool
0.2 m

☐ cm

2 Convert the following measurements.

(a) 260 cm = ☐ m

(b) 3.09 m = ☐ cm

(c) 14.17 m = ☐ cm

(d) ☐ m = 3002 cm

Converting metres and kilometres

An app on Jacob's and Ruby's phones recorded their bike rides. Who cycled the longer distance?

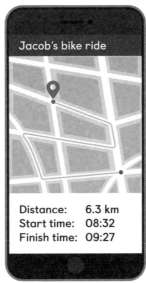

Jacob's bike ride

Distance: 6.3 km
Start time: 08:32
Finish time: 09:27

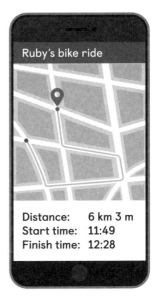

Ruby's bike ride

Distance: 6 km 3 m
Start time: 11:49
Finish time: 12:28

Example

1 km = 1000 m
0.1 km = 100 m
6 km = 6000 m
0.3 km = 300 m

Jacob's bike ride was 6.3 km or 6300 m.

1000 m = 1 km
100 m = 0.1 km
10 m = 0.01 km
1 m = 0.001 km

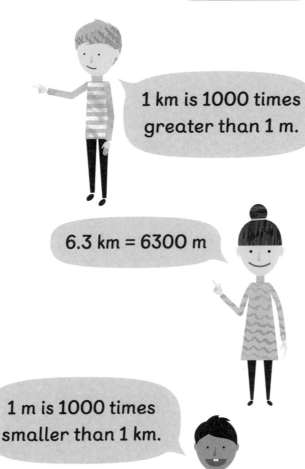

1 km is 1000 times greater than 1 m.

6.3 km = 6300 m

1 m is 1000 times smaller than 1 km.

6000 m = 6 km
3 m = 0.003 km
6000 m + 3 m = 6003 m

6003 m = 6.003 km

Ruby's bike ride was 6003 m or 6.003 km.

6300 m > 6003 m
6.3 km > 6.003 km
Jacob cycled the longer distance.

Practice

1 The children cycled the following distances.

(a) Convert the distances into metres.

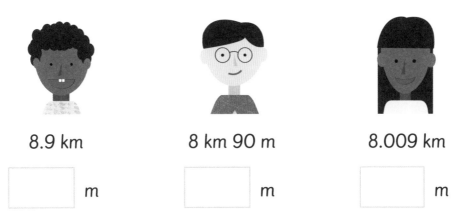

8.9 km

[   ] m

8 km 90 m

[   ] m

8.009 km

[   ] m

(b) Put the distances in order from greatest to smallest.

[   ] , [   ] , [   ]

greatest ⟶ smallest

2 Convert the following distances.

(a) 6.1 km = [   ] m

(b) 2050 m = [   ] km

(c) 13.45 km = [   ] m

(d) 21456 m = [   ] km

Converting grams and kilograms

Starter

The mass of a newborn giant panda is about 100 g. The mass of an adult giant panda is about 100 kg.
How many times greater is the mass of an adult giant panda compared to a newborn giant panda?

Example

1 kg = 1000 g
10 kg = 10 000 g
100 kg = 100 000 g

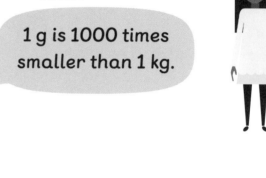

1 kg is 1000 times greater than 1 g.

1 g is 1000 times smaller than 1 kg.

$$100 \text{ g} = \frac{100}{1000}$$

$$= 0.1 \text{ kg}$$

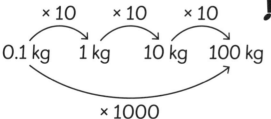

$$\overset{\times 10}{\overset{\frown}{}} \quad \overset{\times 10}{\overset{\frown}{}} \quad \overset{\times 10}{\overset{\frown}{}}$$

0.1 kg   1 kg   10 kg   100 kg

× 1000

100 kg is 1000 times greater than 100 g.
The mass of an adult giant panda is 1000 times greater than the mass of a newborn giant panda.

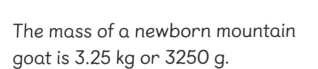

The mass of a newborn mountain goat is 3.25 kg. How many grams is that?

1 kg = 1000 g
3 kg = 3000 g
0.1 kg = 100 g
0.2 kg = 200 g
0.01 kg = 10 g
0.05 kg = 50 g

3.25 kg = 3250 g

The mass of a newborn mountain goat is 3.25 kg or 3250 g.

Practice

1 Convert the mass of each animal to grams.

(a)

3.8 kg

[   ] g

(b)

8.7 kg

[   ] g

(c)

3.44 kg

[   ] g

(d)

0.98 kg

[   ] g

2 Convert the following masses.

(a) 1.1 kg = [   ] g

(b) 8.05 kg = [   ] g

(c) [   ] kg = 4007 g

(d) [   ] kg = 3785 g

Converting litres and millilitres

Starter

Holly wants to make a jug of tropical punch using the following recipe.
What is the total volume of tropical punch she will make?

Tropical Punch

230 ml	pineapple juice
1.4 l	orange juice
360 ml	mango juice

Example

Start by making all the units of measurement the same.

Convert 1.4 l to ml.

1 l = 1000 ml
0.1 l = 100 ml
0.4 l = 100 ml × 4
= 400 ml

1.4 l = 1400 ml

230 ml + 1400 ml + 360 ml = 1990 ml

1000 ml = 1 l
100 ml = 0.1 l
10 ml = 0.01 l

How many litres is 1990 ml?

900 ml = 0.1 l × 9
= 0.9 l

90 ml = 0.01 l × 9
= 0.09 l

1990 ml = 1 l + 0.9 l + 0.09 l
= 1.99 l

Holly will make 1990 ml or 1.99 l of tropical punch.

Practice

1 Find the total volume in millilitres.

(a)

Water 810 ml

Water 1.7 l

Water 0.9 l

☐ ml

(b)

Water 1.05 l

Water 0.75 l

Water 1.1 l

☐ ml

2 Convert the following measurements.

(a) 3000 ml = ☐ l

(b) 5.6 l = ☐ ml

(c) 1230 ml = ☐ l

(d) 8.07 l = ☐ ml

Converting minutes and seconds

Starter

Jacob wants to make a soft-boiled egg.
He looks online to find out how long to boil the egg for.

Boil for 5 minutes 20 seconds.

Boil for $5\frac{1}{2}$ minutes.

Boil for 5.4 minutes.

Are there differences between the times Jacob finds online?

Example

1 min = 60 s
5 min = 60 s × 5
    = 300 s
5 min 20 s = 300 s + 20 s = 320 s

Convert the lengths of time into seconds.

1 min = 60 s
$\frac{1}{2}$ min = 30 s
5 min = 300 s
$5\frac{1}{2}$ min = 330 s

$\frac{1}{2}$ min or 0.5 min is 30 s.

1 min = 60 s
0.1 min = 6 s
0.4 min = 6 s × 4
= 24 s

5 min = 300 s
5.4 min = 300 s + 24 s
= 324 s

0.4 min or $\frac{4}{10}$ min = 24 s

The times that Jacob finds online are all different.

Practice

1 Convert these cooking times into seconds.

(a)

7 min

☐ s

(b)

16 min

☐ s

(c)

$4\frac{1}{4}$ min

☐ s

(d)

3 min 36 s

☐ s

(e)

8.6 min

☐ s

(f)

10.4 min

☐ s

2 Convert the following times.

(a) 240 s = ☐ min

(b) 405 s = ☐ min ☐ s

(c) 6.8 min = ☐ s

(d) $7\frac{1}{4}$ min = ☐ s

Converting units of time

Starter

Ravi accidentally started the stopwatch on his phone.
He pressed stop when he realised it was on.
Is it possible to write the time shown in different ways?

08 18 36 03
Days Hours Mins Secs

Example

We can show the hours
as a part of a day.

1 day = 24 h

18 hours is $\frac{18}{24}$, $\frac{3}{4}$ or 0.75 of a day.

We can write the time as 8.75 days 36 minutes 3 seconds.

We can show the minutes
as part of the hours.

1 h = 60 min

36 minutes is $\frac{36}{60}$, $\frac{6}{10}$ or 0.6 of an hour.

We can write the time as 8 days 18.6 hours 3 seconds.

We can show the seconds
as part of the minutes.

1 min = 60 s

3 seconds is $\frac{3}{60}$, $\frac{1}{20}$ or 0.05 of a minute.

We can write the time as 8 days 18 hours 36.05 minutes.

Practice

1 Show the times as fractions of minutes.

(a)

(b)

(c)

□ □/□ min   □ □/□ min   □ □/□ min

2 Show the times as fractions of hours.

(a) 3 h 10 min = □ □/□ h   (b) 10 h 18 min = □ □/□ h

(c) 13 h 48 min = □ □/□ h   (d) 17 h 54 min = □ □/□ h

3 Show the times as fractions of days.

(a) 2 days 8 h = □ □/□ days

(b) 6 days 16 h = □ □/□ days

Review and challenge

1 The table shows the number of comic books some children own.
If the mean number of comic books owned by each child is 14,
how many comic books must Ravi own?

Child	Lulu	Sam	Ruby	Oak	Holly	Ravi
Number of comic books	21	13	12	21	8	

Ravi owns [ ] comic books.

2 The pie chart shows the number of people who went to the local
swimming pool last week.
360 people went to the swimming pool over 5 days.

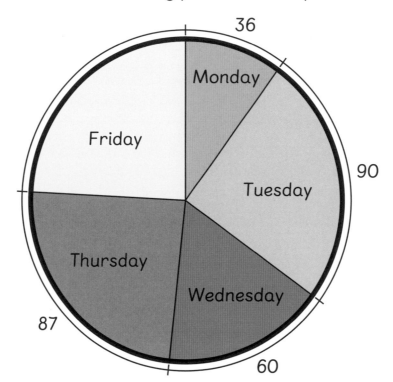

(a) How many people went to the swimming pool on Friday? [ ]

(b) A quarter of the people who went to the swimming pool
over the 5 days went on which day? [ ]

3 The Boeing 747-400 and Airbus A380 are large passenger aeroplanes. The line graph shows the distance the aeroplanes travelled over a number of hours.

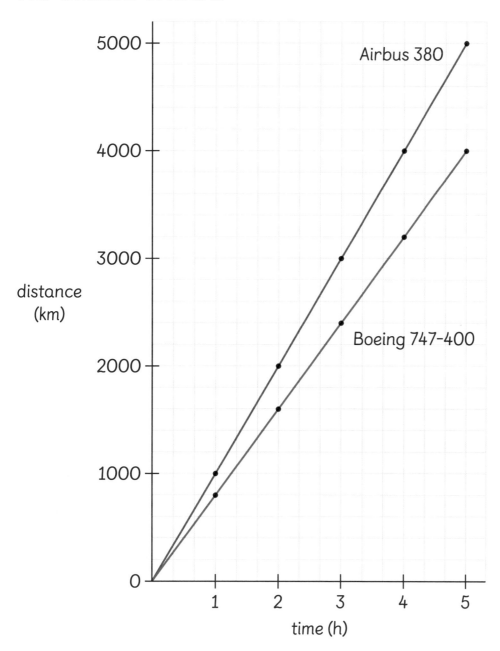

(a) The Boeing 747-400 travelled ☐ km after 4 hours.

(b) After 3 hours, the Airbus A380 travelled ☐ km more than the Boeing 747-400 travelled.

(c) If the aeroplanes continued to fly at the same speed for a total of

7 hours, the difference in the distance travelled would be ☐ km.

4 Convert the following measurements to centimetres.

(a) ————————————— 50 mm

[ ] cm

(b) ——————————— 36 mm

[ ] cm

(c) ————————— 44 mm

[ ] cm

(d) ————————— 29 mm

[ ] cm

5 Convert the following measurements to metres.

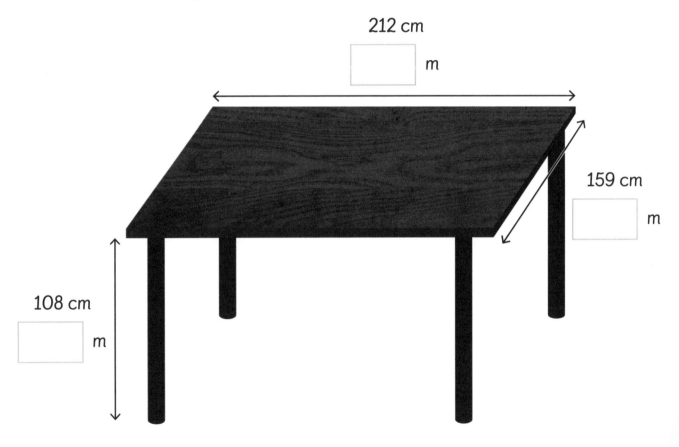

212 cm

[ ] m

159 cm

[ ] m

108 cm

[ ] m

6 Convert the following distances.

(a) 4000 m = [ ] km

(b) 6.7 km = [ ] m

(c) 7089 m = [ ] km

(d) 5.002 km = [ ] m

7 Convert the following masses.

(a) 5000 g = [ ] kg = [ ] kg [ ] g

(b) [ ] g = 8.5 kg = [ ] kg [ ] g

(c) [ ] g = [ ] kg = 6 kg 40 g

(d) 5013 g = [ ] kg = [ ] kg [ ] g

8 Convert the following measurements.

(a) 3000 ml = [ ] l = [ ] l [ ] ml

(b) [ ] ml = [ ] l = 9 l 100 ml

(c) [ ] ml = 7.01 l = [ ] l [ ] ml

(d) [ ] ml = 2.012 l = [ ] l [ ] ml

9 Convert the following times.

(a) 3 days = [ ] h

(b) 6.5 h = [ ] min

(c) 32.2 min = [ ] s

(d) 3.4 min = [ ] s

10 The table shows the number of tries different rugby teams scored in a game. The mean number of tries scored by all of the teams is 13. Team F scored 3 more tries than Team E.
Complete the table.

Team	Team A	Team B	Team C	Team D	Team E	Team F
Number of tries	16	9	11	13		

Answers

Page 5   **1** 4 + 5 + 3 = 12, 12 ÷ 3 = 4, mean = 4   **2** 5 + 5 + 3 + 3 = 16, 16 ÷ 4 = 4, mean = 4   **3** mean = 3

Page 7   **1** mean = 4   **2** mean = 8.2   **3** mean = 7.4

Page 9   **1** Answers will vary.

	Packet A	Packet B	Packet C
1	30	31	29
2	29	28	33
3	27	31	32

2 Even though the number of peanuts in each packet may be different, the manufacturers will want customers to receive a similar amount of peanuts every time they buy a bag. It is unlikely customers would be happy with a bag containing 1 peanut!

Page 13   **1**   **2**

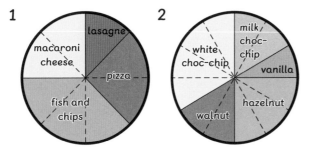

Page 17

Number of pets	1	2	3	4	5
Number of pupils	20	15	10	10	5

Page 20   **1**

Type of book	Percentage of all books
comics	10%
fiction	40%
reference books	20%
non-fiction	30%

Page 21   **2 (a)** The mass of the lettuce Ruby used was 35 g.   **(b)** The mass of the carrots Ruby used was 175 g.   **(c)** The mass of the onion Ruby used was 35 g.   **(d)** The mass of the tomatoes Ruby used was 315 g.

Page 23   **1** The car travelled at 100 km per hour during the first 2 hours.   **2** 1 h   **3** The car was driving at 50 km per hour for 3 hours.

Page 26 **1 (a)**

Time	08:30	09:00	09:30	10:00	10:30	11:00	11:30	12:00	12:30
Number of bins	0	50	100	150	200	200	250	300	350

(b) (i) By 10:30, 200 rubbish bins had been collected. **(ii)** By 12:30, 350 rubbish bins had been collected. **(iii)** At 10:30, the workers stopped collecting rubbish bins and had a break.

Page 27 **2 (a)**

Time	09:00	10:00	11:00	12:00	13:00	14:00	15:00	16:00	17:00
Number of people: Helix	0	100	200	300	400	500	500	600	700
Number of people: Vortex	0	50	100	150	200	250	300	350	400

(b) (i) 150 **(ii)** 50 **(iii)** 1 h

Page 29 **1**

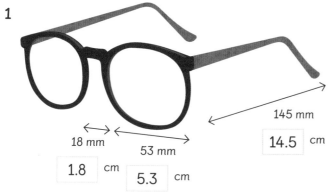

145 mm

14.5 cm

18 mm

53 mm

1.8 cm

5.3 cm

2 (a) 72 mm = 7.2 cm **(b)** 4.5 cm = 45 mm **(c)** 10.7 cm = 107 mm **(d)** 209 mm = 20.9 cm

Page 31 **1 (a)** 430 cm **(b)** 460 cm **(c)** 520 cm **(d)** 162 cm **(e)** 20 cm **2 (a)** 260 cm = 2.6 m **(b)** 3.09 m = 309 cm **(c)** 14.17 m = 1417 cm **(d)** 30.02 m = 3002 cm

Page 33 **1 (a)** 8900 m, 8090 m, 8009 m **(b)** 8.9 km, 8 km 90 m, 8.009 km **2 (a)** 6.1 km = 6100 m **(b)** 2050 m = 2.05 km **(c)** 13.45 km = 13 450 m **(d)** 21 456 m = 21.456 km

Page 35 **1 (a)** 3800 g **(b)** 8700 g **(c)** 3440 g **(d)** 980 g **2 (a)** 1.1 kg = 1100 g **(b)** 8.05 kg = 8050 g **(c)** 4.007 kg **(d)** 3.785 kg = 3785 g

Page 37 **1 (a)** 3410 ml **(b)** 2900 ml **2 (a)** 3000 ml = 3 l **(b)** 5.6 l = 5600 ml **(c)** 1230 ml = 1.23 l **(d)** 8.07 l = 8070 ml

Page 39 **1 (a)** 420 s **(b)** 960 s **(c)** 255 s **(d)** 216 s **(e)** 516 s **(f)** 624 s **2 (a)** 240 s = 4 min **(b)** 405 s = 6 min 45 s **(c)** 6.8 min = 408 s **(d)** $7\frac{1}{4}$ min = 435 s

Page 41 **1 (a)** $5\frac{1}{2}$ min **(b)** $3\frac{1}{4}$ min **(c)** $8\frac{1}{5}$ min **2 (a)** 3 h 10 min = $3\frac{1}{6}$ h **(b)** 10 h 18 min = $10\frac{3}{10}$ h **(c)** 13 h 48 min = $13\frac{4}{5}$ h **(d)** 17 h 54 min = $17\frac{9}{10}$ h **3 (a)** 2 days 8 h = $2\frac{1}{3}$ days **(b)** 6 days 16 h = $6\frac{2}{3}$ days

Page 42 **1** Ravi owns 9 comic books. **2(a)** 87 **(b)** Tuesday

Answers continued

Page 43   **3 (a)** The Boeing 747–400 travelled 3200 km after 4 hours. **(b)** After 3 hours, the Airbus A380 travelled 600 km more than the Boeing 747–400 travelled. **(c)** If the aeroplanes continued to fly at the same speed for a total of 7 hours, the difference in the distance travelled would be 1400 km.

Page 44   **4 (a)** 5 cm **(b)** 3.6 cm **(c)** 4.4 cm **(d)** 2.9 cm

5

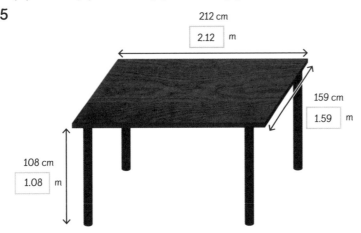

212 cm
2.12 m

159 cm
1.59 m

108 cm
1.08 m

6 (a) 4000 m = 4 km **(b)** 6.7 km = 6700 m **(c)** 7089 m = 7.089 km **(d)** 5.002 km = 5002 m

Page 45   **7 (a)** 5000 g = 5 kg = 5 kg 0 g **(b)** 8500 g = 8.5 kg = 8 kg 500 g
(c) 6040 g = 6.04 kg = 6 kg 40 g **(d)** 5013 g = 5.013 kg = 5 kg 13 g
8 (a) 3000 ml = 3 l = 3 l 0 ml **(b)** 9100 ml = 9.1 l = 9 l 100 ml **(c)** 7010 ml = 7.01 l = 7 l 10 ml
(d) 2012 ml = 2.012 l = 2 l 12 ml **9 (a)** 3 days = 72 h **(b)** 6.5 h = 390 min **(c)** 32.2 min = 1932 s
(d) 3.4 min = 204 s **10**

Team	Team A	Team B	Team C	Team D	Team E	Team F
Number of tries	16	9	11	13	13	16